A TREATISE
ON THE
YOGA PHILOSOPHY

A TREATISE
ON THE
YOGA PHILOSOPHY

N. C. PAUL

GYAN

Published by

GYAN

Gyan Publishing House
5, Ansari Road
Daryaganj, New Delhi-110002
Phone: 011-47034999, 9811692060
E-mail: books@gyanbooks.com

Distribution Network
gyanbooks.com
India, USA, Canada, UK, Australia

ISBN: 978-93-6780-418-6 (PB)

First Published, 1851

2nd Impression 2024

Printed at: Gyan Press, Delhi.

A TREATISE ON THE YOGA PHILOSOPHY
Author: N. C. PAUL

A TREATISE

ON THE

YOGA PHILOSOPHY,

BY

N. C. PAUL, G. B. M. C.,
Sub-Assistant Surgeon.

(SECOND EDITION.)

BENARES:

PRINTED BY E. J. LAZARUS AND CO., MEDICAL HALL PRESS.

1882.

PREFACE.

The present Treatise contains the theory and practice of the Yoga, one of the six systems of docrtine held by the Hindus. The Yoga treats of various processes, by which the Hindu Ecstatici acquire the power of abstaining from eating and breathing for a long time, and of becoming insensible to all external impressions.

The Hindu mystics (yogís) who practise yoga, retire into subterranean retreats (guphá), they abstain from common salt, and are extremely fond of milk, on which they chiefly live: they are nocturnal in their habits, keeping retired in the day; they are slow in their motions, and torpid in their manners; they eat and walk during the night. They practise two postures, termed Padmásana, and Siddhásana, with a view to respire with the least possible frequency. They also dread the rapid changes and inclemencies of the weather.

When the yogís are able to practise the above quiescent postures for the period of two hours, they commence to practise Pránáyáma, a stage of self-trance which is characterised by profuse perspiration, tremblings of the system, and a sense of lightness of the animal œconomy. They next practise Pratyáhára, a stage of self-trance in which they have the functions of the senses suspended. They then practise Dharana, a stage of self-trance in which sensibility and voluntary motion are suspended, and the body is capable of retaining any given posture, the mind being said to be quiescent in this stage of self-trance.

The Yogís, after attaining the stage of Dharana (cataleptic condition), aspire to what is termed Dhyána, a stage of self-trance in which they pretend to be surrounded by flashes of eternal light or electricity, termed Ananta-jyotí, (from two Sanskrit words signifying endless or all-pervading light), which they say is the universal soul. The Yogís in a state of Dhyána are said to be clairvoyant. The Dhyána of the Yogís is the Turyá avasthá of the Vedantists—the ecstacy of the Physician, the self-contemplation of the German mesmerisers, and the clairvoyance of the French philosophers.

Samádhi is the last stage of self-trance. In this state the yogis, like the bat, the hedgehog, the marmot, the hamster, and the dormouse, acquire the power of supporting the abstraction of atmospheric air, and the privation of food and drink. Of samádhi or human hybernation there have been three cases within the last 25 years. The first case occurred in Calcutta, the second in Jesselmere and the third in the Punjab. I was an eye-witness of the first case.

Of samádhi there are two varieties, termed Samprajna and Asamprajna. Colonel Townsend, who could stop the motion of his heart and arteries at pleasure, and could die or expire when he pleased, and again revive, was a case of Samprajna samádhi.

The Jesselmere, the Punjabí, and the Calcutta yogís, who assumed a death-like condition by swallowing the tongue, and who could not revive of themselves at pleasure, were cases of Asamprajna samádhi, as they were all resuscitated by others who drew the buried tongue out of the fauces and restored it to its normal place.

On account of the real obscurity of the nature of the Yoga philosophy, and of my utter ignorance of the Sanskrit language, in which all the standard works on Indian mysticism are written, I must crave some indulgence if I have failed to do full justice to the subject of self-trance as practised by the cold-blooded and hybernating philosophers of the East.

A TREATISE

ON THE

YOGA PHILOSOPHY

BEFORE entering on the consideration of the elements of human hybernation or Yoga, it may not be altogether uninteresting to give a full account of the nature of the expired air, which the Sanskrit authorities term Prána.

The expired air contains more caloric and more watery vapour, is more elastic, and is of less specific gravity than the inspired air. The average temperature of the expired air is 99·5 F.

The average quantity of watery vapour expired in 24 hours by an adult, in temperate climates, is 7,819,222 grains. The bulk of carbonic acid in the 100 parts of the expired air, varies, according to different authorities, as shewn by the table following:—

Authorities.	*Average percentage of carbonic acid by volume.*
Prout, ...	3·45.
Coathupe, ...	4·02.

Thompson, ...	4· 16.
Vierordt, ...	4· 334.
Brunner and Valentine, ...	4· 380.

The quantity of carbonic acid evolved during the day is greater than what is excreted during the night.

For every 12 volumes of carbonic acid evolved during the day, 10 are exhaled during the night. The quantity of carbonic acid evolved in respiration is considerably increased after a full meal. Hence, moderation in diet, termed Mitáhára, is recommended to persons who practise the suspension of the breath. Sequin found that when he was in a state of repose, and fasting, he vitiated only 1,210 cubic inches of oxygen, while, during digestion, this bulk was increased to between 1,800 and 1,900 cubic inches.

With a view to expire less carbonic acid, many faqírs fast during the day and take one moderate meal during the night. These are called Naktabhojí.

Exercise increases the amount of carbonic acid in the expired air in a given time. Aware of this fact, the ancient Hindu philosophers prescribed slow movements to such as wanted to exhale less carbonic acid.

Yogís are recommended to move slowly in order to render their respiration less frequent.

TEMPERATURE.

Human beings deteriorate a greater quantity of air in a cold than in a warm medium; that is to say they, exhale more carbonic acid in a cold atmosphere than in a hot one. Hence the Yogis are recommended to dwell, like the burrowing animals, in subterranean retreats which are remarkable for possessing a uniform temperature. The nearer the temperature of the external air is to the animal heat, the less is the quantity of carbonic acid in the expired air. Hence the appetite for food at the equator is less keen than in the polar regions. The appetite for food is in proportion to the quantity of carbonic acid exhaled during a given time. In a confined atmosphere less carbonic acid is evolved than in the free ventilated air. Hence a Yogí delights to live in a guphá (subterranean cell) having a small door which is blocked up with clay by his assistant.

LOUD SPEAKING.

The amount of carbonic acid exhaled in a given time is greater in loud speaking than in a state of silence. Hence a Yogí is recommended to practise Maunavrata,—taciturnity, or the vow of silence.

MENTAL LABOUR.

Mental labour diminishes the quantity of carbonic acid in the expired air. Hence the Yogís are recommended to avoid physical exertions, and to engage in meditation.

MENTAL ABSTRACTION.

When the mind is abstracted from its functions the amount of carbonic acid is lessened. Hence the Yogís are recommended to fix their sight on the tip of the nose or upon the space between the eye-brows. These peculiar turns of the axes of vision suspend the respiratory movements and generally produce hypnotism. This process is termed Trátaka in Sanskrit.

REST.

The quantity of carbonic acid exhaled in a given time is less in a state of rest than in one of exercise. Hence the Yogís are recommended to sit in the two tranquil and quiescent postures termed the Siddhásana and Kamalásana, of which a circumstantial account will be given while treating of human hybernation.

The longer the state of rest is continued the less is the quantity of carbonic acid evolved from the gradual decrease of the number of respirations. This is better illustrated by the following paragraph quoted from a standard work on Natural History.

"In a specimen of Bombus terrestris, which remained at rest for about half an hour, the respirations had become deep and laboured, and were continued regularly at about fifty-eight per minute. At the expiration of one hundred and forty minutes, during which time the insect remained in a state of repose, the respirations were only forty-six per minute. At the expiration of a hundred and eighty minutes the respirations were no longer perceptible."

As the respirations are fewer in a given time, in persons of sedentary habits, the desire for food is proportionally less keen. Owing to this circumstance, individuals leading a sedentary life are subject to an infinite variety of diseases. A studious man digests badly because he exhales a very small quantity of carbonic acid, owing to the diminished number of respirations dependent on intense mental application and on a state of repose.

Milk diet is well suited to sedentary habits, and generally supersedes the employment of purgatives, emetics and cordials, which are in such general vogue in the treatment of diseases arising from sedentary habits.

INFLUENCE OF DRYNESS AND MOISTURE ON THE EXPIRED AIR.

Human beings exhale more carbonic acid in a dry atmosphere than in a moist one.

INFLUENCE OF HEIGHT OF PLACES.

The exhalation of carbonic acid is greater at the level of the sea than on mountains.

INFLUENCE OF RADIATION AND VAPORIZATION ON THE EXPIRED AIR.

On being exposed to the open air in a carriage or on the deck of a ship, human beings exhale more carbonic acid than usual, from the more active radiation and evaporation from the animal economy.

INFLUENCE OF CONDUCTORS AND NON-CONDUCTORS ON THE EXPIRED AIR.

When we are surrounded by non-conductors, we exhale less carbonic acid, if the atmosphere be cold, than when surrounded by conductors. Hence dealers in metallic utensils consume more food during the winter. A true Yogí is directed not to touch metals of any description. It may be observed that hybernating animals are covered with non-conductors during their long hybernal sleep. Hence the more warmly we are clad, the less is the quantity of carbonic acid evolved, and the less, consequently, is the demand for food.

INFLUENCE OF THE DRINKING OF COLD WATER ON THE EXPIRED AIR.

Those who are accustomed to drink large quantities of cold water, exhale more carbonic acid than those who drink a small quantity of the liquid. A Yogí is recommended to take a small quantity of water to quench his thirst. I have known a native to abstain altogether from water, and to maintain sound health at the same time.

INFLUENCE OF ALCOHOLIC LIQUORS ON THE EXPIRED AIR.

The use of alcoholic liquors causes a considerable diminution in the amount of carbonic acid given out. The Augharhs, a sect of Hindu faqirs, consume a large quantity of alcoholic liquor in the course of the 24 hours.

INFLUENCE OF WEIGHT ON THE EXPIRED AIR.

Persons who are heavy exhale more carbonic acid than those who are comparatively light. Hence the Yogis extenuate their systems, restrain their passions, and subdue their vicious natures, by a parsimonious use of food. Abstinence favours longevity, by diminishing the waste of matter. With frugal fare, St. Anthony lived 105 years; James the Hermit, 104; Arsenius, tutor of the Emperor Arcadius, 120; Simon the Stylite, 112; and Romauld, 120. These Persons took but very little food. Cassian assures us that the common rate, for 24 hours, was 12 ounces of bread and a sufficiency of pure water.

On analysis, 12 ounces of bread will be found to consist of—

Water,	...	2304	Grains.
Carbon,	...	1534.8	do.
Oxygen,	...	1524	do.
Hydrogen,	...	205.2	do.
Nitrogen,	...	72	do.
Salts,	..	120	do.

From the above analysis of the food of the forementiond long-lived individuals, it appears that they consumed a little more than 1500 grains of carbon in 24 hours, and that they respired less than 6 times per minute, as shewn by the table following :—

Number of respirations per minute.	Percentage of carbonic acid in the expired air.	Volume of expired air in a minute.	Volume of Carbonic acid in the expired air in a minute.	Volume of Carbonic acid in each expiration.	Weight of Carbon exhaled in 24 hours, in Grains.
6.	5. 70.	183.	10· 431.	1· 738.	1943· 67
12.	4. 10.	366.	15· 006.	1· 250.	2798· 18
24.	3. 3.	732.	24· 156.	1· 006.	4501· 13
48.	2. 9.	1464.	42· 456.	0· 884.	7911· 08
96.	2.7.	2928.	79· 056.	0· 823.	14772· 22

Abstinence diminishes the number of respirations; it diminishes the waste of body; it promotes longevity.

According to the Hindu Rishis, whatever prolongs the interval (Kumbhaka) promotes longevity. The term Kumbhaka means the interval between an inspiration (púraka) and an expiration (rechaka.) The terms Púraka, Kumbhaka, and Rechaka are frequently met with in almost all the sacred writings of the Hindus. The object of the púraka, (the inspired air) is called Apána, and that of the rechaka (the expired air) is called Prána. The cessation of an expiration constitutes death, and the retention of same life. The suppression of expiration constitutes Pránáyáma, a practice to which the Hindu pretends to acquire ashtasiddhi (eight consummations), and to overcome death. It is the daily practice of the Brahman mendicants who aspire to human hybernation or Yoga.

The stoppage of the respiratory moments (Pránáyáma), or rather the prolongation of the interval (Kumbhaka) has a remarkable effect upon the quantity of carbonic acid in the expired air. Vierordt has made four series of experiments, in order to ascertain the extent of this influence upon the quantity of carbonic acid evolved from the lungs. In the first series, he shut his mouth, and held his nose from 20 to 60 seconds, the longest period he could continue the experiment, and then made the deepest possible inspiration. In the second series, he made the deepest inspiration possible, and then suspended the respiratory movements for a longer or shorter time, at the termination of which he made the deepest expiration. This experiment he was able to prolong to 70, 90, and even 100 seconds.

In the third series, he made an ordinary inspiration before suspending the respiratory movements, and, after this suspension had continued for different periods up to 30 seconds, he made an ordinary expiration. The fourth series of experiments which he performed was to ascertain the period of time, after the stoppage of the respiratory movements, when the percentage of carbonic acid becomes uniform in the different parts of the lungs and air; and this, he found, took place after 40 seconds.

He has arranged the results of the first three series of experiments, in several tables, exhibiting the difference between the percentage and absolute quantity of carbonic acid gas in the expired air, at different periods after the suspension of the respiratory movements, under the circumstances mentioned, and when the respiratory movements proceed in the normal manner. In the first series of experiments, the percentage of carbonic acid in the expired air, after the respiratory movements had been suspended 20 seconds, was higher by 1·73 than when these movements were normal. But the absolute quantity of carbonic acid evolved from the lungs had diminished by 2·642 cubic inches, and at the end of 55 seconds its percentage had increased 2·32; but its absolute quantity had diminished to the extent of 12·382 cubic inches per minute. When the respirations are 3 in number per minute, the percentage of carbonic acid may be reckoned 5·83, and the absolute quantity of the gas in the expired air, 5·33,445 cubic inches in a minute.

When there is but one respiration per minute, the percentage of carbonic acid in the expired air may be reckoned at 6·42, and the absolute quantity of carbonic acid, 1·9581 cubic inches per minute.

In the second series of experiments, where the deepest possible inspiration preceded, and the deepest possible expiration followed the suspension of the respiratory movements, the above quantity of carbonic acid evolved from the lungs for the first 15 seconds, was somewhat more than what there would have been, had these movements preceded. But after this it began to diminish; and when the respiratory movements had been suspended for 95 seconds, it was diminished to the extent of 14·078 cubic inches.

At the end of 100 seconds the percentage of carbonie acid was 3·08 above the normal quantity in ordinary respiration. In the third series of experiments, the carbonic acid in the expired air at the end of 30 seconds, was 1·555 per cent above the normal quantity. When the respirations were 2 in number per minute, the percentage of carbonic acid in the expired air was 5·65.

The normal number of respirations per minute is 12; the average bulk of each expiration is 30·5 English cubic inches; and the normal percentage of carbonic acid is 4·1, by volume.

From the above experiments it is evident that the absolute quantity of carbonic acid evolved from the lungs in a given time, is less in retarded than in normal expiration, and that the percentage of carbonic acid is greater in retarded than in normal expiration.

The exhalation of carbonic acid from the lungs is materially diminished by the inaudible and frequent repetition of certain words, such as Om, Bam, &c., &c. The inaudible pronunciation of Om, the sacred triliteral monosyllable, diminishes the absolute quantity of carbonic acid in the expired air a given time. This constitutes the Japa of Pranava (or

Oṃ). Next to abstinence, Japa ranks in importance. A Dandí who repeats Om twelve thousand times every day, in an inaudible voice, generally lives upon a small quantity of food.

The following words are endowed with the property of inducing sleep, by diminishing the exhalation of carbonic acid :—Soham, Om, Bam, Lam, Ram, Yam, Bam, Ham, &c., &c. The word Om, which, for one, has the property of diminishing the quantity of carbonic acid evolved from the lungs during a given time, is employed to designate the Supreme Being. The pronunciation of this word, which prolongs the Kumbhaka, or interval between an inspiration and expiration, is monopolized by the Bráhman tribe of the Hindus. A boy put himself to sleep, says Dr. Radcliff, by pronouncing the word *cup* 450 times. Any word which prolongs the Kumbhaka (interval), when pronounced slowly and distinctly, may be selected as a hypnotic word. Such a word is *cup*, the pronunciation of which threw the Christian boy into a condition of hypnotic sleep. Japa is one of the most essential ceremonies of Yogís. Counting their rosary is also a very common practice of Yogìs. The aerial Bráhman of Madras, who, practised the suspension of breath (pránáyáma), counted his beads while he maintained the aerial posture, with his hand resting upon a Yoga-danda or staff; and Parama Swatantra Purushánanda Brahmachárì, who practised Yoga towards the latter end of the 18th century at Benares, and slept upon a bed of iron spikes, was given to counting his beads. Amongst the orthodox Hindus the counting of the sacred beads leads to indigestion and costiveness. Many of the noted Japís of Benares cannot digest more than 8 ounces of solid food, which is usually dál and átá.

When the same air is breathed more than once, the quantity of carbonic acid in the expired air is increased. Allen and Pepys state that air passed 9 or 10 times through the lungs contains 9·5 per cent. of carbonic acid.

Mr. Coathupe found the average quantity of carbonic acid in air where warm-blooded animals had been confined until they were becoming comatose, to be 10·42 per cent., whereas, if they were allowed to remain in it until they had become asphyxiated, it contained 12·75 per cent.

The act of breathing the same air more than once is known to the Yogís, who call it the Pránápána Yoga. This is one of the easiest methods of effecting self-trance. Whatever tends to increase the absolute quantity of carbonic acid evolved from the lungs, induces the system to absorb a proportionately increased quantity of oxygen in a given time. For every grain of oxygen that is absorbed, 2·54391 grains of normal blood are decomposed.

Animals which breathe rapidly, consume much oxygen, exhale much carbonic acid, and possess a higher temperature than those which breathe more slowly. The temperature of a child, whose respirations are more frequent than those of an adult, and who can less easily bear hunger, is 102·5 F.; and that of an adult, who requires less nourishment than the former, is 99·5 F. A bird dies from want of food on the third day. Its heat is 106· to 109·

3

The serpent, which, when placed for an hour under a receiver, consumes scarcely so much oxygen as to enable the resulting carbonic acid to be detected, lives for three months, and even longer, without food. The Yogí, like the serpent, endures the privation of air, water, and food, by diminishing his respirations through the practise of Hatha and Rája Yoga, of which a full account will be given in the sequel.

According to the Hindu Rishis, there are five stages of the suppression of respiratory movements. They are as follows; 1. Pránáyáma; 2. Pratyáhára; 3. Dhárana: 4. Dhyána; and, 5. Samádhi.

The following table shows the duration of the inspiration, interval, and expiration, of each of the above stages of the suspensation of the respiratory movements.

DURATION, IN SECONDS.

	Inspirations.	*Interval.*	*Expirations.*
Pránáyáma ...	12 seconds.	324 seconds.	24 seconds.
Pratyáhára ...	do.	648 do.	do.
Dhárana	do.	1296 do.	do.
Dhyána	do.	2592 do.	do.
Samádhi	do.	5184 do.	do.

THE NORMAL NUMBER OF INSPIRATIONS DIFFERS, IN DIFFRENT ANIMALS, AS SHOW BY THE FOLLOWING TABLE.

Names of animals.	*Normal number of inspirations per minute.*
BIRDS.	
Pigeon	34
Common fowl	30
Duck	21
Heron	22
MAMMALIA.	
Monkey	30
Man	12
Guinea pig	36
Dog	28
Cat	24
Goat	24
Rabbit	36
Horse	16
REPTILE RACE.	
Tortoise	3

Of all the above animals the tortoise has the least respiration. It is endowed with the power of supporting the abstraction of atmospheric air and of enduring a suspended respiration (Pránáyáma). It also lives to a great age. One instance is recorded of a tortoise having lived 110 years. It is more tenacious of life, it is notorious for enduring long abstinence, and is composed and tranquil in its manners and habits. It can refrain from eating and breathing for a great part of the year. This animal retires under ground about the middle of November, and comes forth again about the middle of April. It therefore sleeps five months in the year; and during this long hybernal repose it neither breathes nor eats. It sleeps a great part of the summer, it retires to rest before every shower of rain, and does not move at all on wet days. When it first awakes from its winter sleep it discovers but little inclination for food, but in the height of summer it grows voracious. As the summer draws to a close, its appetite, however, declines, so that for the last six weeks in autumn it hardly eats at all. Milky plants are its favourite nourishment. It is, further, insensible to severe wounds.

The Lacerta Palustris is another animal of a similar nature. This creature lives on insects, and hybernates like the land turtle. Common salt is highly poisonous to it, and it dies on being immersed in salt water. It is remarkable for reproducing different parts of the body when deprived of them by accident. I believe this circumstance first attracted the attention of a European medical practitioner in Great Britain, who discovered the new plan of treating Phthisis pulmonalis by enjoining abstinence from common salt. It is by observing a diet similar to that of this reptile, that the Yogís of India have learned the hygienic property of abstinence from common salt. Many faqírs of India abstain from common salt for years together.

The winter dormitory of a Yogí may be compared

to the hybernaculum of a land turtle. The Himalayan marmot, which has a small respiration, hybernates five months in the year. Its respiration is very nearly suspended during hybernation. The evolution of carbonic acid ceases with the subsidence of the animal heat to that of the atmosphere. And to this circumstance the endurance of the total abstraction of atmospheric air, and of food and drink, may be fairly attributed.

Amongst the circumstances which favour hybernation the chief are as follows.

1.—Abstinence. This renders the system more susceptible of the influence of cold; it induces the loss of animal temperature, which subsides to that of the external atmosphere, and produces sleep. Religious fasting has been practised by most nations from the earliest times. Pythagoras fasted for no less than 40 days, and Christ abstained from food and drink for as many days together.

Fasting is a common practice amongst the Hindus. Widows of the superior castes, who are forbidden to marry, are enjoined to fast two days every month, in addition to other fasts, which are oppressively numerous in India, and more especially at Benares, the focus of Hindu superstition.

A faithful Hindu widow, who observes all fasts prescribed by the śástras, and abstains from the indulgence of sexual appetite, generally enjoys good health; and instances of longevity amongst abstinent and continent Hindu widows are not very uncommon at Benares. The longevity of Hindu widows is, in fact, proverbial. It were, indeed, to be desired that the moderation in diet which ensures long life, should be practised by Europeans visiting India, as such persons fall, in great numbers, victims to repletion.

2.—Sheltered situations, as caverns, burrows, &c., &c. These secure hybernating animals from extreme vicissitudes of weather. The guphá, or subterranean retreat, of an Indian Yogí is nothing but an imitation of the winter hybernaculum of the land turtle. The guphá is as indispensably necessary to the Yogí for the practice of Yoga as the cavern is for their winter rest to some of the hybernating animals.

3.—A state of rest or repose is indispensably necessary to hybernation. Many insects reduce their number of respirations by a state of repose. A Yogí who practises suspension of the breath, resorts to tranquil postures, called the Siddhásana and Kamalásana,—the influence of which on the expired air may be more readily imagined than described. A German physiologist alone could do justice to them, by analyzing the air contaminated by a Yogí accustomed to sit in one of these postures for more than 12 hours in the day.

4.—Confined atmosphere also conduces to hybernation. This is better secured by burrows and caverns, which the hybernating animals construct with such ingenuity as to allow of no free ventilation. The Yogí's guphá is so constructed that there is no ventilation, and no disturbance from light and sound.

5.—Non-conductors of heat are essentially necessary to hybernation. Hybernating animals in general make use of hay, straw, cotton, wool, dry leaves of various plants, &c., &c., for beds, in order to prevent the radiation of the earth's temperature. A Yogí, imitating them, prepares his beds from kuśa grass, cotton, and the wool of sheep.

6.—Aliments. The softest vegetables and the lightest animal food are indispensably necessary to hybernation. According to the Hindu Rishis, the chief aliments that conduce to human hybernation are rice, wheat, barley, múng (Phaseolus mungo), milk, sugar, honey, ghí, butter, &c. In addition to the foregoing aliments, a Yogí indulges in the following vegetables :—Boerhaavia diffusa alata (Punarnavá), Jussieu repens, (Hilamochiká), Chenopodium album (vástuká), Cassia sophera (kálakásundá), Amaranthus spinosus (kánttánatiyá), and Tricosanthes Dioica (Pátola). Of pungent aliments he takes only ginger. He regards common salt as highly prejudicial to health. He abstains from this condiment all his life. He also abstains from acid and pungent articles of diet. Flesh, fish, wine, oil, mustard, onions, garlic, and carrots are forbidden to such as intend to lead a religious, moral, intellectual, or hybernal life. Rice, barley, and wheat constitute the chief articles of food of some of the burrowing animals that pass the winter in a torpid state. The marmot, which is distinguished for its long hybernal sleep, is extremely fond of milk. The badger, which passes the greatest part of the winter in a half torpid state, is fond of honey. The turtle, which abstains from eating and breathing for a great part of the year, is fond of milky plants, such as lettuce, dandelions, sow thistles, &c., &c. The Lacerta Aquatica, which is noted for repairing the loss of its legs, tail, and eyes, and which hybernates, dies when immersed in salt water.

From the above observations it is quite evident the Yogí's selection of aliments has been the result of ages of observation of the habits of temperance amongst torpid animals.

Colonel Townsend, an English officer of excellent natural parts, and of great honour and integrity, could die or expire when he pleased, and again revive. He observed the strictest regimen, living on the softest vegetables and the lightest animal food, drinking asses' milk daily, even in the camp, and, for common drink, Bristol water. By an abstemious course of diet he could suspend the respiration and pulsation, and thereby assume a condition similar to death, or the samádhi of the Indian faqírs. Low diet and a state of composure or rest were the principal means employed by the English officer to assume this death-like appearance. The faqír, who was buried alive for 40 days, in the time of Runjeet Singh, and then exhumed, alive, lived entirely upon milk previous to his burial, and abstained from food, drinks, and air, all the time he was buried. To all intents and purposes he hybernated. A faqír, who hybernated in Jesselmere, lived entirely upon milk.

The above facts establish, beyond a doubt, the property, in milk, of conducing to hybernation. All the profane and sacred writing of the Hindus extol milk as an aliment favouring longevity. I believe it is to the highly hygienic property in milk that the cow owes its sanctity amongst the Hindus, whose unparalleled benevolence to the animal is notorious.

All hybernal aliments diminish the exhalation of carbonic acid from the lungs. They therefore diminish the waste of the animal economy.

The following table shows the relative waste of the body from different varieties of diet.

Names of diet.	*Specific number, indicating waste in a given time.*
Vegetable diet ...	1000
Mixed do. ...	1445
Animal do. ...	2367

Without a few remarks, the above table will not be well understood. If a man, living on vegetables, loses 1000 grains in weight in a given time, the same man will lose 1445 grains of his weight during the same time, while living upon mixed diet ; and 2367 grains while living upon animal food.

A studious man digests badly when he lives upon mixed or animal food. But he digests the hybernal aliments with ease. With milk diet he can undergo mental labour which would he painful and injurious to digestion, should he live upon animal or mixed diet. Milk is the normal food of an intellectual man. Mental labour, when indulged in after meals of mixed or animal diet, is the prolific source of an infinite variety of diseases. To painters, engravers, poets, mathematicians, and scientific men in general, the nature of whose avocations requires fixed attention and mental abstraction, milk is admirably adapted.

The following table shows the analysis of milk.

Cow's-milk, as analysed by Liebig.	100 *grains.*	1000 *grains.*	14400 *grains, or* 1 *seer.*	28800 *grains, or* 2 *seers.*
Water	87· 080	870· 80	12539· 520	25070· 940
Carbon	6· 982	69· 82	1005· 408	2010· 816
Hydrogen ...	1· 144	11· 44	164· 736	329· 472
Nitrogen ...	· 520	5· 20	74· 880	149· 760
Oxygen	3· 649	36· 49	525· 456	1050· 912
Salts and earth	· 625	6· 25	50· 000	180· 000

Rice is another article of diet used by the Yogís of India. Its composition is shown in the table following.

Rice.	100 *grains.*	1000 *grains.*	14400 *grains, or* 1 *seer.*
Water	7· 6	76·	1094· 4
Carbon	42· 1036	421· 036	6062· 9184
Hydrogen ...	5· 754	57· 54	828· 576
Nitrogen	1· 268	12· 68.	182· 592
Oxygen	42· 8745	428· 744	9173· 576
Salts and earths,	· 4	4·	57· 6

Wheat is another staple article of diet of Yogís. Its composition is as follows.

Wheat.	100 *grains.*	1000 *grs.*	14400 *grs. or* 1 *seer.*
Water	10·	100·	1440·
Carbon	40· 557	405· 57	5840· 108
Hydrogen	5· 53	55· 3	796· 32
Nitrogen	2· 149	21· 49	308· 556
Oxygen	39· 759	397· 59	5724· 366
Salts and earths	2·	20·	288·

Barley is another article of Yogí's diet. The Emperor Akber, who was noted for justice and moderation, lived upon barley and anethum sowa. According to Dr. Beekman and Bonssingault, barley, dried at 212° F., contains 2·02 per cent. of nitrogen. According to the latest authority, it has the following composition.

Barley.	100 *grains.*	1000 *grs.*	14400 *grs.*, *or* 1 *seer.*
Water...........	9· 37	93· 7	1349· 28
Carbon	44· 32	443· 2	6382· 08
Hydrogen	2· 38	23· 8	342· 72
Nitrogen	1· 8	18·	259· 2
Oxygen	40· 47	404· 7	5827· 28
Salts and earths	1· 66	16· 6	239· 04

Meat, which the Yogís abstain from, has the following composition.

Fresh meat.	100 *grains.*	1000 *grs.*	14400 *grs.*, *or* 1 *seer.*
Water...........	75· 012	750· 12	10801· 2
Carbon	12· 972	129· 72	1867· 99
Hydrogen	1· 897	18· 97	273· 19
Nitrogen	3· 762	37· 62	541· 75
Oxygen	5· 31	5· 31	764· 64
Salts and earths	1· 057	10· 57	152· 23

The numerical proportion of carbon to oxygen, in carbonic acid, is as 1 to 2·666. Carbonic acid that is thrown out from the lungs and the skin, arises from the combination of the carbon of the aliments with the inspired oxygen. When the oxygen is deficient in the aliment, its carbon, in order to be converted into carbonic acid, requires more oxygen from the atmospheric air which can only be accomplished by increasing the number of respirations.

The following table shows the numerical proportion of carbon to oxygen, in different aliments referred to in the foregoing tables.

Aliments.	*Numerical proportion of carbon to Oxygen.*
Fresh meat ...	1 to ·409
Milk ...	1 „ ·522
Barley ...	1 „ ·913
Wheat ...	1 „ ·98
Rice ...	1 „ 1·001

Animal flesh, when used as an aliment, requires more atmospheric oxygen, and hence it is necessary for a carnivorous animal to accelerate respiration by motion. A tiger, which lives entirely upon flesh diet, moves to and fro even when confined in an iron cage, in order to consume the more oxygen from the air. For an amount of meat containing one grain of carbon, the animal most inhale 2·257 grains of atmospheric oxygen.

One living upon cow's-milk must inhale 2·144 grains of atmospheric oxygen for a quantity of the nutritious fluid containing one of carbon. He should be less active than one living upon flesh diet. A person who lives upon barley consumes 1·753 grains of atmospheric oxygen for a quantity of the aliment containing one grain of carbon. He that lives upon wheat consumes 1·686 grains of atmospheric oxygen for a quantity of the aliment yielding one grain of carbon. One living upon rice requires 1·665 of atmospheric oxygen for a quantity of the aliment containing one grain of carbon.

The following table shows the relative quatity of atmospheric oxygen, in grains, required for one grain of carbon of different aliments.

Aliments.	*Relative Quantity of atmospheric oxygen for each alimental grain of carbon.*
Meat ...	2· 257 grains.
Milk ...	2· 144 "
Barley ...	1· 753 "
Wheat ...	1· 686 "
Rice ...	1· 665 "

An aliment is more or less stimulant to the circulating system, according to the more or less quantity of nitrogen contained in a given weight of the substance, as shown by the table following.

Azotized aliments.	*Quantity*	*Quantity of Nitrogen.*
Fresh meat ...	1000	37· 62
Wheat ...	do.	21· 49
Barley ...	do.	18· 00
Rice ...	do.	12· 68
Fresh cow's-milk,	do.	5· 20
Fresh asses'-milk.	do.	2· 63

From the above table it is evident that asses'-milk is the least stimulant to the circulating system ; and, owing to this cirumstance, Colonel Townshend, who used asses'-milk habitually, acquired the power of expiring and reviving when he pleased.

Woman's milk contains 1·9516 per cent. of nitrogen. 1000 parts of this milk contain 1·9516 of nitrogen. It is the lightest of all animal aliments. A child at the breast enjoys a longer repose, in consequence of the low stimulating nature of woman's milk, which is the only nourishmet it takes until it is weaned.

The hybernal aliments, such as barley, rice, wheat, sugar, ghee, milk, &c., &c., promote longevity, increase power and strength. They are pleasing to the palate, nourishing, permanent, and congenial to the body. According to the Bhagavad gítá, all aliments which are neither too bitter, too saltish, too hot, too pungent, too astringent, nor too inflammable or heat ing, are regarded as *satya guni* food. They are said to be palatable, nourishing, permanent, and congenial to the body.

SLEEP.

As Yoga, or human hybernation, is nothing more than prolonged sleep, it may not be altogether uninteresting to discuss the subject of somnolency before we enter the difficult subject of self-trance practised by the Indian faqirs. Sleep may be defined the repose of the organs of sense and motion. "It is of inestimable value to man. It knits up the ravelled sleeve of care. It is the death of each day's life. It is sore labour's bath. It is the balm of hurt minds, and chief nourisher in life's feast."

The duration of sleep in manhood is from 4 to 6

hours per day. It is longer with the child at the breast than with one that is weaned. It is longer with boys and girls than in the case of adults; and longer with adults than with the aged.

There are instances on record, of individuals sleeping for weeks, months, nay even for years.

"Samuel Chilton, a labourer, aged about 25, residing at Timsbury near Bath, was accustomed to fall into a sleep from which no one could rouse him till after a month's time, during which he neither ate nor drank. Once he slept for seven weeks, during which he made water once and had one evacuation."

"There lived in the parish of Cortachy, in the county of Forfar, between 1819 and 1834, a certain female, Euphemia Lindsay, commonly known through the most of Forfarshire by the appellation of sleeping Effie. Her peculiarities were as remarkable as those of any one who has appeared in the annals of human history. She was addicted to wandering, and commonly left her home about the time when other people retired to rest, and during the night would frequently wander from twelve to fifteen miles. It was remarked that when she took these nocturnal journeys she was sure shortly afterwards to fall into sleeping fits; and it was no unusual thing for her to sleep two or three weeks without awaking. In the winter of 1820 she slept five weeks, and during the spring of 1825 she slept six weeks and three days, which was the longest sleep she had been known to take. She never touched her store of provisions during the time she slept."

During sleep the temperature of the body is

diminished, the number of pulsations diminished, and the respirations less frequent and audible. During deep sleep there are about 22 pulsations and 6 respirations per minute. Sleep is prolonged in proportion as the animal heat subsides to that of the surrounding atmosphere.

A deep and perfect sleep (sushupti) has been aptly defined a temporary cessation of all the functions of animal life, viz., of thought, sensation, mental emotion, and all their combinations and modifications. In *sushupti* the soul is extricated from terrestrial bonds, and man is free from all sins.

Yoga has been differently defined by different authorities. Some have defined it mental abstraction; some have defined it silent prayer; some have defined it the union of the inspired to the expired air; some have defined it the union of mind to soul. But by Yoga I understand the art of suspending the circulation and respiration. Yoga is chiefly divided into *Rája Yoga* and *Hathx Yoga*. I shall first consider *Rája Yoga*.

Rája Yoga consists of eight stages, viz., Yama, Niyama, Aśana, Pránáyáma, Pratyáhára, Dháraná, Dhyána, and Samádhi.

Yama.—Under this term the practice of the five acts of restraint is included, viz., Ahinsá, (absence of violence or curelty to living creatures, universal innocence), Asteya (avoidance of theft), Satya (truth), Brahmacharya (chastity), and Aparigraha (disinterestedness, or non-acceptance of gifts).

Under the head of Yama some of the best moral maxims of all religions are evidently included.

Niyama.—After practising Yama, a Yogí practises Niyama. Under Niyama are comprehended; S'aucha (purity, personal cleanliness), Santosha (contentment, patience under injuries), Tapasya (devotion, self-mortification, self-denial), Swádhyáya (knowledge of nature and of soul), and I'śwara pranidhana (adoration of one Supreme Being, the Creator, the Preserver, and Destroyer of the world).

A'sana.—This is a fixed attitude of intense meditation. It is the third stage of Yoga. There are many ásanas or postures, in which the Yogí is directed to sit while he engages in Yoga, or the art of reducing or suspending the functions of respiration and circulation. Of these ásanas the most important are the Siddhásana and the Padmásana.

Without the practice of ásana, Yoga cannot be practised. By the practice of ásana the Yogí is supposed to secure immunity from certain diseases.

By practising successfully the two postures, Padmásana and Siddhásana, one can easily attain the 7th and 8th stages of Yoga, viz., Dhyana and Samádhi. The Siddhásana may be thus practised. Place the left heel under the anus and the right heel in front of the genitals; fix the sight upon the space between the eye brows, or the seat of the phrenological power, Individuality, and, while in this motionless attitude, meditate upon the syllable Om, a mysterious word, the frequent inaudible repetition of which is said to ensure release from worldly existence.

The second posture is the Padmásana, which is thus practised. Place the left foot upon the right thigh, and the right foot upon the left thigh; hold with the right hand the right great toe, and with the left hand the left great toe, (the hands coming from behind the back and crossing each other); rest the chin on the interclavicular space, and fix the sight on the tip of the nose.

The Siddhásana and Padmásana are both tranquil and quiet postures, favoring a tranquil circulation and slow respiration. In these postures the Yogís sit and pronouuce inaudibly the hypnotic syllable Om, and meditate upon it, in order to tranquillize circulation and retard the respiratory movements. By persevering practice, the Yogís prolong the duration of the above-named postures, and, in proportion as they continue these attitudes, they diminish the quantity of their aliments. They reside in their subterranean retreats, called *guphás,* after they have become adept in the practice of these postures. There they live upon hybernal aliments, a circumstantial account of which has been recorded in the preceding pages.

When a Yogí, by practice, is enabled to maintain himself in one of the above-mentioned postures for the period of three hours, and to live upon a quantity of food proportional to the reduced condition of circulation and respiration, without inconvenience, he proceeds to the practice of Pránáyáma. This is the fourth stage or division of Yoga. It is the suspension of the respiratory movements, which the Yogís daily practise with a view to purging themselves from minor sins. Like the Himalayan marmot, a Yogí lives in a subterranean retreat, which is contrived with great art, and consists of an oval cavern, large enough to contain two or three individuals, and having a narrow and long passage. The entrance to the *guphá* is very narrow, and is blocked up with clay when the Yogí attains to the state of Samádhi While living in the *guphá*, the Yogí lives upon milk, of which he is extremely fond, and sits and lies upon kuśa grass, blankets, and skins of the stag. Breathing the confined atmosphere of a guphá possessing uniform temperature, he is not troubled by the viscissitudes of the weather to which others are liable. A Yogí is directed to pronounce inaudibly the mantras, Bam, Sam, and Lam, 600 times. He then pronounces Bam, Bham, Mam, Yam, Ram, and Lam, 6000 times. He next pronounces Dam, Dham; Nam, Tam, Tham, Dam, Dham, Nam, Pam, and Pham, 6000 times. He then pronounces inaudibly Kam, Kham, Gam, Gham, Nam, Cham, Chham, Jam, Jham, Nam, Tam, and Tham. He then pronounces inauddibly Am, Ám, Im, Í'm, Um, U'm, Rim, Rím, Lrim, Lrím, Em, Aim, Om, Aum, Am, 6000 times. And lastly he utters inaudibly Hansa 2000 times. He follows this course of japa for some time, in order to reduce his respiration, and thereby enable himself to endure the privation of air for a time without inconvenience. Dr. Grant says that an animal whose respiration is small can endure the total privation of air for a certain period.

He next practises the Yámyásana for the period of three months, in the following manner. He inspires through the left nostril, fills the stomach with the inspired air by the act of deglutition, suspends the breath, and then expires through the right nostril. He next inspires through the right nostril, swallows the inspired air, suspends the breath, and finally expires through the left nostril. By the practice of the Yámyásana the Yogí purifies his system, and is thereby enabled to swallow a large quantity of the inspired air.

Suspension of the breath, or Pránáyáma, cannot be practised by a Yogí who eats more than enough or less than enough; who sleeps too much or who does not sleep at all. A person who is moderate in eating, sleeping, and recreation and exercise, is qualified for the practice of Pránáyáma. He aims at a pure, sublime, and perfect devotion, unalloyed with all selfish consideration. He aspires to an entire disinterested love of God, with a view to obtaining beatitude, or emancipation from terrestrial bonds, technically called *Moksha*. With a view to purify his soul, a Yogí courts silence or taciturnity (maunavrata), tranquillity, repose, solitude, moderation in eating and sleeping; turns away his eyes from terrestrial vanities, and practises the Pránáyáma.

The following are the principal processes of Pránáyáma, selected from different authorities.

PRELIMINARY PROCESS.

Inspire through the left nostril for the period of 3·4128 seconds, suspend the breath for the period of 13·6512 seconds, and then slowly expire for the period of 6·8256 seconds, through the right nostril. Then inspire through the right nostril for the period of 3·4128 seconds, suspend the breath for the period of 13·6512 seconds, and then expire through the left nostril for the period of 6·8256 seconds. Lastly, commence the process with the left nostril in a similar way. This process is to be practised four times in the course of the day, for the period of 48 minutes each time. Continue the process for three months, at the expiration of which attempt to increase gradually the duration of Práṅáyáma until able to practise the following process. Inspire through the left nostril for the period of 13·6512 seconds, suspend the breath for the period of 54·6048 seconds, and then expire through the right nostril for the period of 27·3024 seconds. Next inspire through the right nostril for the period of 13·6512 seconds, suspend the breath for the peiod of 54·6048 seconds, and inspire slowly through the left nostril for the period of 27·3024 seconds, and lastly, inspire through the left nostril once more for the period of 13·6512 seconds. Suspend the breath for the period of 54·6048 seconds, and expire through the right nostril for the period of 27·3024 seconds.

According to some Yogís, Práṅáyáma is of three kinds, the Adhama, Madhyama, and Uttama. The Adhama Práṅáyáma excites the secretion of sweat. It is thus practised. Inspire through the left nostril for the period of 2·5596 seconds, suspend the breath for the period of 10·2384 seconds, and expire through the right nostril for the period of 5·1192 seconds. Next inspire through the right nostril for the period of 2·5596 seconds, suspend the breath for the period of 10·2384 seconds, and expire through the right nostril for the period of 5·1192 seconds. Lastly, inspire through the left nostril for the period of 2·5596 seconds, suspend the breath for the period of 10·2384 seconds, and expire through the right nostril for the period of 5·1192 seconds. The second variety of Pránáyáma is called the Madhyama Pránáyáma. It is attended by convulsive movements of the features. It is thus practised. Inspire through the left nostril for the period of 5·1192 seconds, suspend the breath for the period of 20·4768 seconds, and expire through the right nostril for the period of 10·2384 seconds. Next inspire through the right nostril for the period of 5·1192 seconds, suspend the breath for the period of 20·4768 seconds, and expire through the left nostril for the period of 10·2384 seconds. Lastly, inspire through the left nostril for the period of 5·1192 seconds, suspend the breath for the period of 20·4768 seconds, and expire through the right nostril for the period of 20·2384 seconds. The third or Uttama variety of Pránáyáma raises the Padmásana above the surface of the earth. It is by the successful practice of this Pránáyáma that the aerial Brahman of Madras is supposed to have supported himself in a miraculous posture, which puzzled the ingenuity of the European spectators. It is thus practised. Inspire through the left nostril for the period of 7·6788 seconds, suspend the breath for the period of 30·7152 seconds, and expire through the right nostril for the period of 15·3576 seconds. Next inspire through the right nostril for the period of 30·7152 seconds, and expire through the right nostril for the period of 7·6788 seconds, suspend the breath for the period of 30·7152 seconds, and expire through the left nostril for the period of 15·3576 seconds. Lastly, inspire through the left nostril for the period of 7·6788 seconds, suspend the breath for the period of 30·7152 seconds, and expire through the right nostril for the period of 15·3576 seconds.

There are eight varieties of Kumbhaka which Yogís practise with a view to study the nature of the soul. They are as follows: Súryabhedi, Ujjayí, S'ítkárí, S'ítalí, Bhastriká, Bhrámarí, Múrchchhá, and Kevala Kumbhaka. There are two processes which are essentially necessary for the practise of the above Kumbhakas. These are the Khecharí mudrá, and the Múlabandha.

Khecharí mudrá is the act of lengthening the tongue by incising the frænum linguæ and by constant exercise. A Yogí cuts the frænum linguæ, rubs the tongue with his hands, and milks it. When the tongue gets lengthened by the division of the frænum linguæ and by the milking process, and reaches the gullet, the Yogí, is enabled to shut the rima glottidis by pressing back the epiglottis with the point of the retroverted tongue.

A large and long tongue is indispensably necessary to human hybernation. The turtle, salamander, and guana, which hybernate, have remarkably long and large tongues. A Yogí, by artificial means, lengthens his tongue, turns back the point of it into the gullet, presses the epiglottis, which shuts the rima glottidis, and confines the inspired air within the sytem.

In practising this mudrá, a Yogí fills the lungs and intestines with the inspired air, shuts up all the apertures of body with the waxed cotton balls, assumes the Padmásana. and then shuts the rima glottidis by means of the epiglottis pressed upon by the point of the tongue wedged into the gullet.

By the practice of this mudrá, a Yogí is supposed to be able to overcome death. He becomes a poet or a prophet at will. He becomes a pure soul, and can penetrate the secrets of the past, the present, and the future. Without it he can never be absorbed into God. By the pratcice of this mudrá he becomes insensible, to heat and cold, to pleasure and pain, and holds communion with the "Supreme, Incorruptible, Invisible, Eternal, Inexhaustible, Inconceivable, Omniscient, Omnipresent, and Omnipotent Being," which by the learned is termed the Parama Purusha.

This mudrá removes hunger, thirst, and sleep. The blood of a Yogì who practises this mudrá for the period of 24 years, becomes converted into chyle. The saliva that is sucked or deglutated during the continuance of this mudra, is termed *Amrita*.

Múlabandha is a process by the practice of which an old man becomes a youth. It is thus practised. Place the left foot on the anus, and the right foot in front of the genitals, and breathe the same air over and over again. Or, sit in the posture termed the padmásana, with a cotton ball pressing upon the anus. The Yogí then extends his lower extremities, inspires through the right nostril, rests his chin on his breast, places his forehead on his knees, holds his great toes with his hands, and suspends the breath. When fatigued, he expires through the left nostril, and commences a similar process through the left nostril, and lastly, through the right nostril. This constitutes the *Paśchima tâna* of the Yogí.

The *Súrgabhedi Kumbhaka* consists in inspiring through the right nostril, suspending the breath, and then expiring through the left nostril. In this kumbhaka, inspiration is made through the right nostril. Suspension of the breath is effected by resting the chin on the breast *(jalandara bandka);* and expiration is performed through the left nostril, upon which the hairs of the body become erect. The posture employed in this kumbhaka is the padmásana or sukhásana. By the repetition of this kumbhaka, cephalalgia is relieved, corryza cured, and the worms found in the frontal sinuses are expelled.

Ujjayi Kumbhaka.—By the exercise of this Kumbhaka, a Yogí enhances his personal beauty. It is thus practised. Assume the posture called Sukhásana, render the two nostril free by the first Kumbhaka, inspire through both nostrils, fill the stomach and throat with the inspired air, suspend the breath, and then expire slowly through the left nostril He that practises this Kumbhaka gets rid of pulmonary, cardiac, and dropsical, diseases. By this Kumbhaka a Yogí cures all diseases dependent upon deficient inhalation of oxygen.

Sít kara Kumbhaka.—It is thus practised. Expire through both nostrils, after yawning, (which is a deep and prolonged inspiration,) inspire through the mouth with the two rows of teeth in contact, producing the sound of c. c., suspend the breath, and then expire through the nostrils. This practice increases the beauty and vigour of the body ; it removes hunger and thrist, indolence and sleep; and augments the irritability of the system. By this Kumbhaka a Yogí becomes a cold-blooded and an independent being.

Sítalí Kumbhaka.—It is thus practised. Apply the tip of the tongue to the soft palate, inspire by the combined exertion of the tongue and soft palate, suspend the breath, and expire slowly through both nostrils, after relaxing the whole system. By the uninterrupted practice of this Kumbhaka for the period of one month, a Yogí is said to acquire great tenacity of life, and power of repairing the effects of injury. He becomes proof against all sorts of inflammation and fever. Like crabs, lobster, serpents, lizards, salamanders, toads, frogs, and turtles, which exhibit none of to the phenomena of inflammation, a Yogí becomes a cold-blooded creature, and is exempted from fevers, splenitis, and several organic diseases. He is endowed with the property of casting his skin, and of enduring the privation of air, water, and food. By becoming a cold-blooded creature he can the better endure to spend his time in solitude and devotion.

A Yogí who lives entirely upon milk, ghí, and cold water, is competent to practise this Kumbhaka, which promotes a love of study and retirement, and renders the system susceptible of self-trance, a condition in which he is said to be susceptible to peculiar spiritual impressions. By three years' practice of this Kumbhaka, a Yogí is said to hold communion with the Supreme Soul.

It is believed that the serpents cast their skins by the practice of this Kumbhaka. The fact of the cool surface of the skin of a serpent may be attributed to this peculiar mode of respiration. As the serpent has a long narrow tongue, it can easily practise this Kumbhaka by turning its tongue back into the fauces, and inspiring through the nostrils.

The Sítalí Kumbhaka may be regarded as an admirable imitation of the respiration of a serpent, which, of all animals, is the most remarkable for abstinence, and which can endure the privation of food, drinks, and air, for the longest period.

Bhastriká Kumbhaka.—This is the fifth Kumbhaka. It promotes appetite, opens the three superior valves of the intestinal canal, and cures all pulmonary and hepatic diseases. It is an excellent substitute for exercise. The Bhastriká Kumbhaka is thus practised. Place the left foot upon the right thigh, and the right foot upon the left thigh, straighten the neck and back, make the palms of the hands rest upon the knees, shut the mouth, and expire forcibly through both nostrils. Next, inspire and expire quickly until you are fatigued. Then inspire through the right nostril, fill the abdomen with the inspired air, suspend the breath, and fix the sight on the tip of the nose. Then expire through the left nostril; suspend the breath, and expire through the right nostril. It is by this variety of respiration that the chameleon assumes the apparent conditions of plumpness and leanness. This animal becomes plump by inflating its lungs and intestinal canal with the inspired air, and then becomes lean by a single expiration from those organs. The long continued hissing sound which serpents produce to alarm their prey, is effected by the expulsion through their nostrils of a great volume of air taken into the lungs and the intestinal canal by long continued inspiration. It is by taking more air into the system than is employed in oxygenating the blood, that most of the reptiles are enabled to lighten their bodies, and to swim over lakes and rivers, or perform bounding motions on the dry land. The act of taking in more air than is subservient to respiration, is the characteristic feature of all hybernating animals; and the ancient Hindu philosophers, observing this fact in nature, discovered this variety of respiration. An Indian Yogí becomes plump by inflating his intestinal canal with the inspired air, and then lean by expiring the inspired air. He becomes light by introducing a large quantity of the inspired air into his system, and he becomes specifically heavier by compressing the inspired air within the system. Such is the explanation of two of the "perfections" of the Yogí. When a Yogí fills the whole intestinal canal with the inspired air by the practice of this kumbhaka, he is said to acquire the property of casting his skin, and of altering his specific gravity at pleasure.

Bhrámarí Kumbhaka.—It consists in respiring rapidly, with a view to augment the animal heat by quickening the circulation, in the first instance, and thereby to lower the animal heat by profuse perspiration, and when the temperature of the body is reduced indirectly by the rapid and violent respiratory movement, then by suspending the breath. A Yogí seated in one of the tranquil postures, begins to respire through his two nostrils, at first very gradually. In a short time he renders his respirations more and more frequent, until he is bathed in perspiration. He next inspires through both nostrils, and suspends the breath, and then expires slowly.

Murchchhá Kumbhaka.—This inducees fainting. It is thus practised. Sit in the posture of siddhásana, inspire in such a way as to produce the sound of raining, suspend the breath, resting the chin on the breast until you expect fainting, and then expire. Should fainting occur you are certain that the kumbhaka is successfully practised. A Yogí is directed by the Gheranda Sanhitá to inspire in such a way as to produce the sound of raining, to rest his chin on the chest, to suspend the breath, to stop the ears with the fingers, to listen to the sounds of the right ear with the left ear, and to expire (when he ceases to hear any sound,) through the nostrils.

Kevala Kumbhaka.—This is the eighth or last kumbhaka. It cures all diseases, purges from all sins, promotes longevity, removes darkness of mind, enlightens the moral nature, and awakens the soul. It induces what is called Samádhi. This kumbhaka can only be practised by a Yogí who lives for a long time in a subterranean retreat constructed according to the directions laid down in the Yoga S'ástra, who subsists entirely upon milk, and who is well experienced in the knowledge and practice of the foregoing kumbhakas and of the Khecharí mudrá. The Yogí makes 24 incision in the frænum linguæ, each incision being performed on every eighth day. After each incision he milks the tongue for seven days with astringent, oily, and saline substances, twice a day. During six whole months he lives entirely upon milk, and practises the suspension of breath in his subterranean retreat, gradually diminishing the amount of his food. At the approach of winter, when he finds that he can stop the breathing by swallowing the tongue, he lives for about a week on ghí and milk, abstains from all sorts of food for a day or two, fills the stomach and intestines with the inspired air, sits in the posture of siddhásana, takes a deep inspiration, fills the lungs with the inspired air, shuts the rima glottidis with the glottis pressed backward by the point of the tongue swallowed into the fauces, and thus suspends the breath, with his eyes fixed upon the space between the eyebrows.

"A pupa of sphina ligustri, which, in the month of August, immediately after its transformation, weighed 71·1 grains, in the month of April following weighed 67·4 grains; having thus lost only 3·7 grains in the period of nearly 8 months of entire abstinence. The whole of this expenditure had passed off by the cutaneous and respiratory surface. But when the changes in the internal structures are nearly completed, and the perfect insect is soon to be developed, the respiration of the pupa is greatly increased, and gaseous expenditure of the body is augmented in the rates of the volume of its respiration, which is greater the nearer the period of developement. Thus, in the same insect the diminution of weight, which was so trifling during eight months' quiescence and abstinence, amounted, in the succeeding 51 days, to nearly half the original weight of the pupa, since the perfect insect, immeditely after its appearance on the 24th of May weighed only thirty-six grains."

How the Panjábí faqír, by suspending his breath, lived 40 days without food and drinks, is a question which has puzzled a great many learned men of Europe.

If we compare the habits of the hybernating animals with those of the Yogís, we find that they are identically the same; and consequeutly it is no wonder that we hear of a Yogí's abstaining from food for a month or two.

According to S'uka Deva, who is a high authority on the subject of human hybernation, a man is considered an adept in Pránáyáma when he can suspend his respiratory movements for the period of five minutes and twenty-four seconds. A *dandin* states that Pránáyáma consists in the inaudible pronunciation of *om* one thousand times. According to the Kásí Khanda, Pránáyáma consists in the suspension of breath for the period of fifty seconds.

In order to preserve himself from the corruption of the world, to court the delights of solitude and study, and to dedicate his mind to nothing temporal, a Yogí has recourse to Mitáhára and Pránáyáma.

I have already given a full account of Pránáyáma. I shall now describe Mitáhára.

The aliments of man are either primary or secondary. Of the first class are wheat, barley, and rice. These are the staple or substantive aliments, in contradistinction to others which are called secondary. The secondary or adjective articles of diet are chiefly milk, sugar, ghí, honey, múng, and five culinary vegetables. The primary articles of diet are mixed with secondary ones, and constitute the food of man. A Yogí is directed to take 1728 grains of any of the above primary aliments, along with necessary quantities of the secondary ones. A hermit or *vánaprastha* should take 3456 grains of rice, or wheat, or barley, along with the necessary quantities of usual hybernal secondary aliments, while a wordly man must take double the allowance of aliments prescribed to the hermit.

Milk is the only aliment that can be taken by itself, it combining the properties of both classes of aliments. A Yogí should consume as much milk as contains 975 grains of carbon, while a hermit takes as much of that nourishing fluid as contains 1950 grains of carbon; and, lastly, a worldy man must consume a quantity of that nuriment containing 3900 grains of carbon.

The worldly man, in India, from the above statement, is taught to consume, daily, 8 ounces and 1 dram of carbon, with a view to maintain his health. The hermit consumes 4 ounces and 30 grains of carbon; and, lastly, the cold blooded and hybernal philosopher, who is insensible to the stings and motions of sense, is directed to consume two ounces and fifteen grains (Troy weight) of carbon in his hybernal aliments.

Pratyahára.—This is the fifth stage or division of Yoga. It is the suspension of the senses. Dr. Wilson defines Pratyáhára to be control of the senses. A Yogí who lives upon a dish of rice prepared with butter, sugar, and milk, and acquires the properties of gentleness, knowledge, and resignation, practises the suspension of the respiratory movements; and when he suspends the breath for 10 minutes his senses become suspended.

The organs of sense are susceptible of external impressions. The eyes are acted upon by colour, which is of seven sorts, white, blue, yellow, red, green, orange, and variegated. The tongue appreciates savour, which is of six sorts, sweet, acid, saline, bitter, astringent, and pungent. The organ of smell cognises two sorts of odour, fragrance and stench. The organ of hearing takes cognizance of sounds, which, according to the Yogís, are of ten kinds. And the organ of touch perceives the feelings of hardness, softness, roughness, slipperiness, heat, cold, &c., &c. The organs of sense are called the organs of intellect (Buddhíndriya).

A Yogí restrains his senses, just as a tortoise draws in all its members, by the following processes.

1st Process.—Be seated in a quiet and tranquil posture, and fix your sight on the space between the eye-brows, or the seat of the phrenological power termed Individuality. This process is daily practised for the space of 10 minutes, when only the senses are suspended.

2nd Process.—Be seated in a tranquil posture, and fix your sight on the tip of the nose for the space of ten minutes.

3rd Process.—Close the ears with the middle fingers, incline the head a little to the left side, and listen with each ear alternately to the sounds produced by the other ear, for the space of 10 minutes.

4TH PROCESS.—Pronounce inaudibly, twelve thousand times, the mystic syllable, *Om*, and meditate upon it daily, after deep inspirations.

5TH PROCESS.—This is the kapálásana, in which the Yogí maintains an erect posture, with the head resting on the ground.

According to S'uka Deva, a Yogí's senses are suspended when he can suspend the respiratory movements for the period of 10 minutes and 48 seconds. After the restraint of the senses, the Yogí renders his mind tranquil, with a view to adapt it to acquire wisdom *(jnána)*. He brings back the wandering thoughts, and dissolves them in the contemplation of the soul.

Pratyáhára is the preparatory process to Dharaná, which is a steady immovable abstraction, with the breath suspended, the mind collected, and all natural wants subdued. The symptoms of Dharaná closely resemble those of the cataleptic condition of the body.

Dharaná.—This is the sixth stage or division of Yoga. It is the suspension of the operations of the mind. When a Yogí suspends the respiratory movements for two hours, he is said to accomplish the dharaná, which has for its object a tranquillity of mind free from every degree of sensual disturbance.

1ST PROCESS.—Repeat the mystic syllable *Om* 144.000 times in silence, and meditate upon it, and you will suspend the functions or operations of the mind.

2ND PROCESS.—Fix the eyes upon the point of the nose for the period of 2 hours.

3RD PROCESS.—Fix the eyes upon the space between the eye-brows for two hours.

4TH PROCESS.—After a few forcible inspirations, swallow the tongue, and thereby suspend the breath, and suck and deglutate the saliva for two hours.

5TH PROCESS.—Listen to the sounds within the right ear, abstractedly, for two hours, with the left ear.

According to Súka Deva, a Yogí is blessed with a tranquil mind, when his respiratory movements are suspended for the period of 21 minutes and 36 seconds.

Dhyána.—This is the seventh stage or division of Yoga. It is the intense and abstract contemplation of the soul, after the suspension of the operations or functions of the senses and of the mind. It is the suspension of the respiration and circulation for the period of 24 hours.

When a Yogí keeps his head, neck, and body steady, in a state of absolute quietude, and his senses and mind free from sensual and mental excitements, for 24 hours, he is said to be in a state of dhyána. It has for its object the property of awakening the soul.

1ST PROCESS.—Pronounce slowly and inaudibly the mystic syllable *Om* 1,728,000 times, in one position of absolute rest.

2ND PROCESS.—Fix the sight on the tip of the nose for 24 hours.

3RD PROCESS.—Fix the sight on the space between the eye-brows for 24 hours.

During the state of Dhyána, the Yogí acquires

the power of clairvoyance,and is said to hold communion with the Supreme Being.

According to Súka Deva, a man is said to hold communion with the Supreme Being by suspending his respiratory movements for the period of 43 minutes and 12 seconds.

Samádhi.—This the eighth and last division of Yoga. It is a state of perfect human hybernation, in which a Yogí is insensible to heat and cold, to pleasure and to pain, A hybernant Yogí is insensible to blows and wounds. He is insensible to the effects of fire. He is the same in prosperity and adversity. He enjoys an ecstatic condition. He is free from lust, fear, and anger. He is disengaged from all works. He is not affected by honour and dishonour, He looks upon gold, iron, and stones with the same unconcerned eyes. He is the same in love and hatred. He is the same amongst friends and enemies.

As the water of a river beats the shore when there is wind, so the unsteady mind roams with the continuance of respiration. Just as the waves diminish when the air becomes still, so the mind moves not when the respiration ceases. Whatever diminishes the respiration renders the mind calm.

1ST PROCESS.—Practise the Kevala Kumbhaka, of which a particular account has been given in the preceding pages.

2ND PROCESS.—Repeat the mystic syllable *Om* 20,736,000 times, in silence, and meditate upon it.

3RD PROCESS.—Suspend the respiratory movements for the period of 12 days, and you will be in a state of samádhi.

According to Śukadeva, one acquires a perfect condition of human hybernation when one's respiratory movements are suspended for the period of one hour, twenty six minutes, and twenty-four seconds. In a state of human hybernation a Yogí is not poisoned by snake-bites, he remains unaffected by the cutting of weapons, he is not afflicted with pain when brought in contact with fire. Like the hybernating animals, Yogís resist the injuries of weapons and fire. They die not when drowned in water; nor do they dry up when exposed to air. They live without food, water, and air, while in the condition of samádhi. Yogis, like the torpid animals while hybernating, are incapable of committing sin in act, thought, or speech.

A Yogí whose functions of respiration and circulation are suspended, is deprived of the power of committing sin in act, thought, or speech. Samádhi, then, is the total suspension of the functions of respiration and circulation, but not the extinction of those functions.

Professor Wilson explains Samádhi to be the entire occupation of the thoughts by the idea of Brahma (the Supreme Soul), without any effort of the mind.

As I have treated of the various branches of Rája Yoga, by which a Yogí analyses the various corporeal, intellectual, moral, sensual, and religious principles of which man is composed, and by which he segregates or awakens the soul to the contemplation of, and absorption into, the Supreme soul, the Creator, Preserver, and Destroyer of the world,—I will now give a succinct account of Hatha Yoga, which the Panjábí faqír successfully practised before a large concourse of Native and European gentlemen.

HATHA YOGA.

Hatha Yoga treats of the various methods by which one can attain to the state of self-trance, and acquire the power of hybernating.

The Hatha Yogí, like the Rája Yogí, lives entirely upon milk, previously to his acquiring the condition of samádhi or human hybernation. He lives in a *gupha* or subterranean cell, and avoids the society of man. First of all he practises the six purgatory processes. He that can maintain good health on the allowance of two seers of fresh cow's milk in the course of 24 hours, is competent to the practise of the six purgatory processes, which are as follows.

Neti.—This is the first purgatory process. It consists in the act of passing a twisted cord of delicate thread, of two lines in diameter, and eleven inches in length, through one of the nostrils and bringing it out at the mouth. This process is performed alternately through both the nostrils. This is a very easy process.

Dhautí.—This is the act of swallowing a bandage of linen moistened with water, measuring 3 inches in breadth and 15 cubits in length. This is rather a difficult process. But very few faqírs can practise it.

Bastí.—This is the act of inhaling water through the anus, and discharging it from the same aperture. The *holothuria pentactes* practises this process almost every moment of its existence. *Lancet*, 1833-1834, Vol. 2, page 960.

Gajakarma.—This is the act of vomiting a large quantity of water, after filling the stomach and œsophagus with that liquid, by fixing the sight on the space between the eyebrows. This is a very simple process.

Naulí.—This is the alternate exercise of the recti-muscles of the abdomen, while the back and abdomen are straightened. I have seen many faqírs practise this process.

Trátaka.—This is the act of fixing the sight on the tip of the nose, or upon the space between the eyebrows. until tears come into the eyes. A Hatha Yogí next practises the following mudrás or immovable postures.

Khecharí Mudrá.—This is the act of swallowing the tongue, with a view to producing suspension of breath.

I quote the following cases of insensibility and suspension of respiration consequent upon this Mudrá.

" I was called," says Dr. Lawe " to a negro child in the town of Sabarra, in Brazil, born in a state of asphyxia. I examined his mouth, found the tongue turned over, and very deep in the fauces. With the intention of removing any foreign matter that might perhaps obstruct the passage of air, I put my finger into the mouth of the infant, and, moving the tongue to draw it forth, the air rushed in forcibly and the child began to cry and to breathe." *Lancet*, 1832-33, Vol. 2, page 361.

The following passage occurs in 'Notices of

Brazil in 1828-29, by the Rev. R. Walsh, L L. D.' In speaking of the foreign slave trade, he remarks:—"The wretched slaves often inflict death upon themselves in an extraordinary manner. They bury their tongue in the throat in such a way as to produce suffocation. A friend of mine was passing when a slave was tied and flogged; after a few lashes, he hung his head, appearing lifeless; and, when taken down, was actually dead. His tongue was found wedged in the œsophagus, so as completely to close the trachea. The slave who, by this action of his tongue, provokes death, hitherto has been supposed to be dead; and in many instances, perhaps without any examination at all, his body has been consigned to the grave." *Lancet*,. 1836-1837, Vol. 2, p. 258.

"Mr. J. T. Batten, of Tooley-street, has forwarded to us the following particulars of his treatment of an infant which had lost all signs of vitality for a space of nearly half an hour directly after its birth:—'Mrs. R. gave birth to the child on the 4th instant. She had previously had three children, each of which, born between the eighth and ninth month, had expired at birth, under similar circumstances, having, however, been left without any efforts at resuscitation. On this occasion, says Mr. B., my determination was to act with the greatest care, so that the chord was not tied until the infant had cried powerfully and its maternal pulsation had ceased. It was at this period that vitality seemed to cease. The moment placental circulation stopped, the crying rapidly lost power: presently respiration failed, and animal heat receded, so that just three minutes after birth every symptom of animation subsided. The skin was of a cadaverous aspect, while the surface of the body was quite cold, and the heart and lungs were left without a vestige of impulse. I first applied friction to the chest by means of gin, which happened to be in the room; and having directed it to be wrapped in flannel, and instructed the nurse to procure hot water, my next step was to inflate the lungs; which, having no apparatus at hand, was effected by my mouth, but with a result entirely fruitless so far. A warm bath was now formed, of the temperature of my own blood, in which the child was immersed; and the fat-like matter being washed from the surface of its body, artificial respiration was again resorted to; this was easily effected, as just described, during the pressure of the fingers upon the œsophagus and nostrils,—of course alternately emptying the lungs by a similar process. But nothing seemed of any service; and a quarter of an hour had now elapsed since the signs of life had subsided. Having introduced my fingers upon the epiglottis, which seemed to rest in a rather tenacious manner in its situation, and raised its apex a little, artificial respiration was again persevered in; when, to my surprise and satisfaction, signs of returning life showed themselves. The surface of the thorax and the lower extremities seemed to resume their natural colour, animal heat gradually returned, and an occasional movement supervened. Twenty-five minutes had now elapsed, and a full space of half an hour had passed before the vital functions were decidedly restored." *Lancet*, 1833-34, Vol. 2, page 861.

The common practice of quieting infants, employed by nurses, consists in thrusting into their mouths a bag made of wash-leather, containing sugar. It may be considered as a substitute for the *Khechari Mudrá*. See page 36.

There are two authentic cases of human hybernation on record.

I.—The account of the Faqír of the Panjáb is thus described in the words of Dr. McGregor. "A Faqueer, who arrived at Lahore, engaged to bury himself for any length of time, shut up in a box, and without either food or drink. Runjeet naturally disbelieved the man's assertions, and was determined to put them to the test. For this purpose the Faqueer was shut up in a wooden box, which was placed in a small apartment below the middle of the ground; there was a folding door to his box, which was secured by a lock and a key. Surrounding this apartment there was the garden-house, the door of which was likewise locked; and outside the whole, a high wall, having its door-way built up with bricks and mud. In order to prevent any one from approaching the place, a line of sentries was placed, and relieved at regular intervals. The strictest watch was kept up for the space of forty days and forty nights, at the expiration of which period the Maharajah, attended by his grandson and several of his Sirdars, as well as General Ventura, Captain Wade, and myself, proceeded to disinter the Faqueer. The bricks and mud were removed from the outer door-way; the door of the garden house was next unlocked, and lastly that of the wooden box containing the Faqueer. The latter was found covered with a white sheet, on removing which, the figure of the man presented itself in a sitting posture. His hands and arms were pressed to his sides, and his legs and thighs crossed. The first step of the operation of resuscitation consisted in pouring over his head a quantity of warm water. After this, a hot cake of atta was placed on the crown of his head; a plug of wax was next removed from one of his nostrils, and, on this being done, the man breathed strongly through it. The mouth was now opened, and the tongue, which had been closely applied to the roof of the mouth, brought forward, and both it and the lips anointed with ghee. During this part of the proceeding I could not feel the pulsation of the wrist, though the temperature of the body was much above the natural standard of health. The legs and arms being extended, and the eyelids raised, the former were well rubbed, and a little ghee applied to the latter. The eyelids presented a dimmed, suffused appearance, like those of a corpse. The man now evinced signs of returning animation; the pulse became perceptible at the wrist, whilst the unnatural temperature of the body rapidly diminished. He made several ineffectual efforts to speak, and at length uttered a few words, in a tone so low and feeble as to render them inaudible. When the Faqueer was able to converse, the completion of the feat was announced by the discharge of guns, and other demonstrations of joy. A rich chain of gold was placed round his neck by Runjeet, and ear-rings, bawbles, and shawls were presented to him."

II.—The account of the second Faqír is thus

described, in the words of Lieut. A. H. Boileau. "I have just witnessed a singular circumstance, of which I had heard during our stay at this place, but said nothing about before, the time for its accomplishment not being completed. This morning, however, a man who had been buried a month, on the bank of a tank, near our camp, was dug out alive, in the presence of Esur Lal, one of the ministers of the Muharáwul of Jaisulmer, on whose account this singular individual voluntarily was interred a month ago. He is a youngish man, about thirty years of age, and his native village is within 5 kos of Kurnaul; but he generally travels about the country to Ajmere, Kotah, Indore, &c., and allows himself to be buried for weeks, or months, by any person who will pay him handsomely for the same. In the present instance, the Ráwul put this singular body in requisition, under the hope of obtaining an heir to his throne...... He was buried at Jaisulmer, in a small building about twelve feet by eight, built of stone. In the floor was a hole, three feet long, two and half feet wide, and perhaps a yard deep, in which he was placed, in a sitting posture, sewed up in his shroud, with his feet (or legs) turned inwards towards the stomach, and his hands also pointed inwards towards the chest. Two heavy slabs of stone, six feet long, several inches thick, and broad enough to cover the mouth of the grave, so that he could not escape, were then placed over him, and I believe a little earth was plastered over the whole, so as to make the surface of the grave smooth and compact. The door of the house was also built up, and people were placed outside, that no tricks might be played. At the expiration of a full month, that is to say, this morning, the walling of the door was broken, and the buried man dug out of the grave. He was perfectly senseless, his eyes were closed, his hands cramped and powerless, his stomach shrunk very much, and his teeth jammed so fast together, that they were forced to open his mouth with an iron instrument, to pour a little water down his throat. He gradually recovered his senses, and the use of his limbs, and when we went to see him, was sitting up, supported by two men, and conversed in a low feeble tone of voice.... Cornet McNaghten, ... assistant to the agent to the Governor-General in Rajpootana, put his abstinence to the test at Pookur, by suspending him, for thirteen days, shut up in a wooden chest...... The man is said, by long practice, to have acquired the art of holding his breath, by shutting the mouth and stopping the interior opening of the nostrils with his tongue...... His powers of abstinence must be wonderful; nor does his hair grow during the time he remains buried. I really believe that there is no imposture in the case."

Both these faqírs were Hatha Yogís. They practised the Khecharí Mudrá successfully, and thereby acquired the power of abstinence from air, water, and food, for a long time.

2.—*Bhúcharí Mudrá.*—This consists in directing the sight to the point of the nose, while seated in the posture called Padmásana. Both the Khecharí and Bhúcharí mudrás produce self-trance in a short time.

3.—*Cháchari Mudrá.*—To practise this mudrá the

sight is fixed on a point three inches in front of the eyes. In this mudrá the sight should be direct, and fixed for a long time. When the Yogí is fatigued, he turns his eyes to the point of the nose, and then to the part between the eyebrows, until self-trance is effected.

4.—*A'gocharí Mudrá.*—This is the method of producing self-trance through the function of hearing. A Yogí who practises this mudrá, plugs the ears with balls of waxed cotton, and listens to the sounds of the left ear with the right ear, bending the head a little laterally, towards the right shoulder, until self-trance is effected.

5 —*Unamaní Mudrá.*—This is the method of suspending the breath, by shutting all the outlets of the body, after a deep inspiration. A Yogí who practises this mudrá successfully, is said to be able to recall the soul, to awaken it, and enjoy heavenly felicity. He needs not prayers nor hymns. He becomes self-tranced.

A Hatha Yogí practises the 4 *bandhas* or restraints, which are as follows :—

1.—*Múlabandha.*—A Yogí practises this bandha by placing his left heel in contact with the anus, or by sitting in the posture of Padmásana, with a cloth ball in contact with the anus, and secured by a bandage.

2.—*Jalandharabandha.*—A Yogí practises this bandha by resting his chin on the interclavicular region, and suspending the breath, after taking a deep inspiration.

3.—*Udyánabandha.*—A Yogí practises this bandha by shutting the mouth, swallowing the tongue, placing the right heel in contact with the epigastric region, and closing the ears, nostrils, and anus, after filling the system with the inspired air.

4.—*Mahábandha.*—In order to practise this bandha, a Yogí places his left foot on the anus, rests his chin on the breast, holds his right foot with his hands extended, and places his forehead in contact with the knees; inspires through the left nostril, fills the stomach and lungs with the inspired air, fixes his eyes on the point of his nose, suspends the breath, and, lastly, expires through the right nostril. He then inspires through the right nostril, suspends the breath, expires through the left nostril, and, finally, breathes through the left nostril, expiring through the right nostril. When one practises this bandha for three successive hours one is said to be an accomplished Yogí, and entitled to practise Samádhi or human hybernation.

OF THE ASHTA SIDDHI, OR EIGHT CONSUMMATIONS.

1, 2—*Animá and Mahimá.*—A chameleon, by merely inspiring air, renders the whole of its body, from the head to the rectum, turgid, round, and plump; and merely by a single expiration of air, the whole of the body again assumes a lank and lean appearance. The lean and lank condition of the system is technically named Animá; and the turgid, round, and plump appearance is denoted by the term Mahimá.

A Yogí, imitating the chameleon, fills his lungs and the whole of the intestinal canal with inspired air, and acquires a plump, round, and turgid appearance (mahimá); and becomes lean and lank again (animá) by a single expiration.

3, 4.—*Laghimá and Garimá.*—The sturgeon, by swallowing great draughts of the atmosphere, distends not only the stomach, but a large bag that communicates with the œsophagus, and thereby becomes specifically lighter, and floats above the surface of the sea. A Yogí, by long practice, acquires the power of swallowing large draughts of the air, and thereby produces a diminution of his specific gravity (laghimá). It is on this principle that the Brahman of Madras maintained himself in an aerial posture. A Yogí acquires an increase of specific gravity (garimá) by swallowing great draughts of the air, and compressing the same within the system.

5.—*Prápti.* – This is the obtaining of desired objects. A Yogí, in a state of self-trance, acquires the power of predicting future events, of understanding unknown languages, of curing divers diseases, of divining the unexpressed thoughts of others, of hearing distant sounds, of seeing distant objects, of smelling mystical fragrant odours, of embracing mystical beautiful woman, and of understanding the language of beasts and birds.

Such is the description of prápti in the several works on Yoga to which I have had access.

6.—*Prákámya.*—By Prákámya is meant the power of casting the old skin and maintaining a youth-like appearance for an unusual period of time. By some writers it is defined to be the property of entering into the system of another. Yayáti, who was old and decrepid, and yet anxious to enjoy sexual appetite, entered into the system of his youngest son, having left his own body. So say the Purânas.

7.—*Vaśitwa.*—This is the power of taming living creatures, or of bringing them under control.

"Pythagoras, who visited India, is said to have tamed, by the influence of his will or word, a furious bear, prevented an ox from eating beans, and stopped an eagle in its flight."

Vaśitwa may be defined to be the power of mesmerising persons by the exercise of the will and of making them obedient to one's own wishes and orders.

Some learned pandits define Vaśitwa to be the restraint of passions and emotions.

8.—*Íśatwa, or Divine Power.*—When the passions are restrained from their desires, the mind becomes tranquil and the soul is awakened. The Yogí becomes full of Brahma (the Supreme Soul). His eye penetrates all the secrets of nature, he knows the events of the past, present, and future; and, when he is not led astray by the temptations of the seven preceding "perfectons," his soul not only holds communion with the invisible, inconceivable, unalterable, omnipresent, omniscient, and omnipotent Being, but he becomes absorbed into the essence of the same. It is commonly supposed that a Yogí who acquires this power, can restore the dead to life.

THE END.

